Reading Shakespeare Today

TWELFTH NIGHT

Elizabeth Schmermund and Dale Robeson

Cavendish Square

New York

Published in 2017 by Cavendish Square Publishing, LLC
243 5th Avenue, Suite 136, New York, NY 10016

Copyright © 2017 by Cavendish Square Publishing, LLC

First Edition

Library of Congress Cataloging-in-Publication Data

Names: Schmermund, Elizabeth, author. I Robeson, Dale, author.
Title: Twelfth Night / Elizabeth Schmermund and Dale Robeson.
Description: New York : Cavendish Square, 2017. I
Series: Reading Shakespeare today I Includes index.
Identifiers: ISBN 9781502623379 (library bound) I ISBN 9781502623386 (ebook)
Subjects: LCSH: Shakespeare, William, 1564-1616. Twelfth night--Juvenile literature.
Classification: LCC PR2837.S34 2017 I DDC 822.3'3--dc23

Editorial Director: David McNamara
Editor: Caitlyn Miller
Copy Editor: Rebecca Rohan
Associate Art Director: Amy Greenan
Designer: Lindsey Auten
Production Coordinator: Karol Szymczuk
Photo Research: J8 Media

Printed in the United States of America

CONTENTS

Introduction

SHAKESPEARE AND HIS WORLD

Mystery shrouds Shakespeare's life and yet, for most of us, the Bard's plays and poems are more familiar than any other author's body of work. Almost everyone has heard of the characters Romeo and Juliet, or of Hamlet's soliloquy on mortality as he holds the skull of Yorick before him. Famous lines such as "To be or not to be: that is the question"; "Friends, Romans, countrymen, lend me your ears"; and "What fools these mortals be!" have entered into our cultural consciousness in a very real way.

William Shakespeare was born in the town of Stratford-upon-Avon in England in April 1564. At the age of eighteen, he married Anne Hathaway, a woman eight years his senior. Together, they had a daughter, named Susanna, followed by the twins Hamnet and Judith. After this, however, Shakespeare's name disappears from historical records until the early 1590s, when he entered history as a member of London's leading acting company, the Lord Chamberlain's Men.

By 1593, William Shakespeare published his first work, a long poem called *Venus and Adonis*, and cemented his literary fame. In 1594, Shakespeare's plays began

This is one of only two known portraits of the famous playwright William Shakespeare painted during his lifetime. Today it is housed in the National Portrait Gallery in London, England.

to appear in print in individual publications, called "quartos," although they were not published under his name until 1598. But while Shakespeare was now at the height of his fame, his life was not immune to tragedy. In 1596, Shakespeare's only son, Hamnet, died at the age of eleven, possibly of the plague. Some scholars believe that *Twelfth Night*, though a comedy, was based in part on Shakespeare's grief over his son's death. While the twins, Viola and Sebastian, are eventually reunited by the end of the play, bringing about its comedic conclusion, *Twelfth Night* begins with the grief that Viola feels when she believes her twin has been lost. Of course, it's the complexity of Shakespeare's plays, such as the hints of tragedy throughout comedies such as *Twelfth Night*, that have enticed audiences for hundreds of years. Shakespeare's world is close enough to our own to elicit our sympathies, and distant enough to create intrigue.

Throughout his lifetime, Shakespeare was best known for crowd-rousing comedies like *The Taming of the Shrew*, *A Midsummer Night's Dream*, *Much Ado About Nothing*, *As You Like It*, and, of course, *Twelfth Night*. Following his death in 1616, at the age of fifty-two, Shakespeare's fame not only endured, but increased. Today, Shakespeare is perhaps best known for his tragedies, including the famous tale of two star-crossed lovers, *Romeo and Juliet*, the tale of the overambitious Scottish general, *Macbeth*, and, of course, the most famous play ever written, *Hamlet*. These tragedies have been adapted around the world for hundreds of years and have resulted in well-loved stage productions, films, movies, operas, and even comic books. Most people around the world have heard of some of Shakespeare's works, even though they were written over four hundred years ago.

In fact, Shakespeare's influence on contemporary culture is so great that we regularly use his words, even though we often aren't aware of it. Shakespeare wrote in Early Modern English—a language very different from the English we speak today. Early Modern English would be very unfamiliar to readers in the twenty-first century, with its use of words like "thou," "thee," "thy," "thyself," and "thine." These words, which mean "you" in various forms, were common during Shakespeare's day but have disappeared from contemporary English. Yet Shakespeare did more than just use the common language of the day—he actually invented over 1,700 words by changing nouns into verbs, connecting different words together, and even coming up with completely original words. Words such as "elbow," "luggage," "swagger," "compromise," "courtship," "critic," "blanket," and "bedroom" were all coined by Shakespeare. In this way, Shakespeare's words influence our lives every day.

Shakespeare's works can be challenging for the modern reader. But if you give his words enough time, they will blossom for you. His comedies are outrageous and bawdy, and his tragedies reveal deep lessons about human nature. Shakespeare's plays were written to be performed; if you have the chance, catch a performance of one of his plays (perhaps *Twelfth Night*), whether at your school, your local theater, or on Broadway. If this proves impossible, as you read, imagine how the characters would swagger and strut across the stage, engaging in sword fights or declaring their love for one another, or speaking cleverly about some confusion known only to the audience. Imagine their colorful costumes and the passion with which the actors (all men during Shakespeare's time) spoke their lines. William Shakespeare's works will come alive again, before your very eyes.

Chapter One

Shakespeare and *Twelfth Night*

S hakespeare's plays were meant to be performed, and he intended them to be performed in the style and tradition of Elizabethan theater. While most of us who know and love Shakespeare's works today first encountered them on the page—that is, printed in a book—reading was not a popular form of entertainment during Shakespeare's era. Gutenberg's printing press, which would revolutionize the distribution of books, was only invented in the mid-fifteenth century. For most people in sixteenth-century England, the best way to be entertained was going to the theater. And Shakespeare was a master of entertainment. His plays are bawdy and include many off-color jokes, sudden plot twists, lively sword fights, and tender romances meant to capture an

This 1650 engraving of London, England, shows the Globe Theatre in the center foreground.

audience's attention. At the Globe Theatre in London, where most of Shakespeare's plays were originally performed, audiences would pay whatever they could afford to watch the Bard's diversions.

Shakespeare's Theater

Today, we sometimes speak of "live entertainment." In Shakespeare's day, of course, all entertainment was live, because recordings, films, television, and radio did not yet exist.

In fact, most communication in those days was difficult. Transportation was not only difficult but slow, chiefly by horse and boat. Most people were illiterate peasants who lived on farms that they seldom left; cities grew up along waterways and were subject to frequent plagues that could wipe out much of the population within weeks.

Money—in coin form, not paper—was scarce and hardly existed outside the cities. By today's standards, even the rich were poor. Life was precarious. Most children died young, and famine or disease might kill anyone at any time. Everyone was familiar with death. Starvation was not rare or remote, as it is to most of us today. Medical care was poor and might kill as many people as it healed.

This was the grim background of Shakespeare's theater during the reign of Queen Elizabeth I, who ruled from 1558 until her death in 1603. During that period, England was also torn by religious conflict, often violent, among Roman Catholics who were loyal to the Pope, adherents of the Church of England who were loyal to the queen, and the Puritans, who would take over the country in the revolution of 1642.

Under these conditions, most forms of entertainment were luxuries that were out of most people's reach. The only way to hear music was to be in the actual physical presence of singers or musicians with their instruments, which were primitive by our standards.

One brutal form of entertainment, popular in London, was bear-baiting. A bear was blinded and chained to a stake, where fierce dogs called mastiffs were turned loose to tear him apart. The theaters had to compete with the bear gardens, as they were called, for spectators.

The Puritans, or radical Protestants, objected to bear-baiting and tried to ban it. Despite their modern reputation, the Puritans were anything but conservative. Conservative people, attached to old customs, hated the Puritans. They seemed to upset everything. (Many of America's first settlers, such as the Pilgrims who came over on the *Mayflower*, were dissidents who were fleeing the Church of England.)

Plays were extremely popular, but they were primitive, too. They had to be performed outdoors in the afternoon because of the lack of indoor lighting. Often the "theater" was only an enclosed courtyard. Probably the versions of Shakespeare's plays that we know today were not used in full, but shortened to about two hours for actual performance.

Eventually more regular theaters were built, featuring a raised stage extending into the audience. Poorer spectators (illiterate "groundlings") stood on the ground around it, at times exposed to rain and snow. Wealthier people sat in raised tiers above. Aside from some costumes, there were few props or special effects and almost no scenery. Much had to be imagined: whole battles might be represented

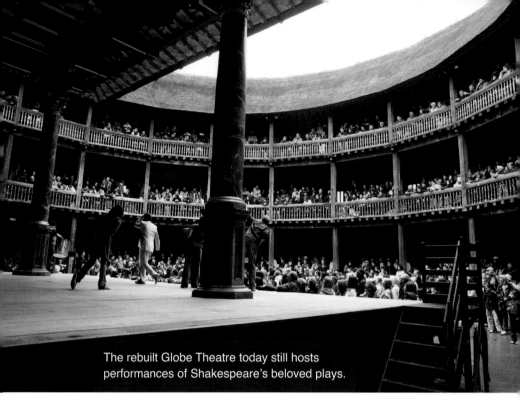

The rebuilt Globe Theatre today still hosts performances of Shakespeare's beloved plays.

by a few actors with swords. Thunder might be simulated by rattling a sheet of tin offstage.

The plays were far from realistic and, under the conditions of the time, could hardly try to be. Above the rear of the main stage was a small balcony. (It was this balcony from which Juliet spoke to Romeo.) Ghosts and witches might appear by entering through a trapdoor in the stage floor.

Unlike the modern theater, Shakespeare's Globe Theatre—he describes it as "this wooden O"—had no curtain separating the stage from the audience. This allowed intimacy between the players and the spectators. The spectators probably reacted rowdily to the play, not listening in reverent silence. After all, they had come to have fun! And few of them were scholars. Again, a play had to amuse people who could not read.

The lines of plays were written and spoken in prose or, more often, in a form of verse called iambic pentameter (ten syllables with five stresses per line). There was no attempt at modern realism. Only males were allowed on the stage, so some of the greatest women's roles ever written had to be played by boys or men. (The same is true, by the way, of the ancient Greek theater.)

Actors had to be versatile, skilled not only in acting, but also in fencing, singing, dancing, and acrobatics. Within its limitations, the theater offered a considerable variety of spectacles.

Plays were big business, not yet regarded as high art, sponsored by important and powerful people (the queen loved them as much as the groundlings did). The London acting companies also toured and performed in the provinces. When plagues struck London, the government might order the theaters to be closed to prevent the spread of disease among crowds. (They remained empty for nearly two years from 1593 to 1594.)

As the theater became more popular, the Puritans grew as hostile to it as they were to bear-baiting. Plays, like books, were censored by the government, and the Puritans fought to increase restrictions, eventually banning any mention of God and other sacred topics on the stage.

In 1642, the Puritans shut down all the theaters in London, and in 1644, they had the Globe demolished. The theaters remained closed until Charles's son King Charles II was restored to the throne in 1660 and the hated Puritans were finally vanquished.

By then, however, the tradition of Shakespeare's theater had been fatally interrupted. His plays remained popular, but they were often rewritten by inferior dramatists, and

Shakespeare's Globe Theatre

THE GLOBE THEATRE in London, England, is Shakespeare's theater in a very real way—although it is not the same theater in which his plays were originally performed.

The Lord Chamberlain's Men built the Globe Theatre on Maiden Lane (now Park Street) in Southwark, London, in 1599. As Shakespeare was, by this point, a shareholder in the acting troupe, he became a shareholder of the Globe as well, owning 25 percent of it. Unfortunately, during a staging of *Henry VIII* in 1613, the theater went up in flames. According to legend, a cannon used in the play set fire to the wooden beams supporting the stage. It was rebuilt the following year. (Shakespeare didn't live long enough to see many of his plays produced in this new theater; he passed away two years later, in 1616.) The second Globe Theatre, unfortunately, did not last too long either. It was destroyed in 1645, although modern scholars don't know exactly why.

A modern version of the theater, now called Shakespeare's Globe, opened in 1997. It was built according to the known specifications of the original Globe and is situated about 750 feet (229 m) away from the original theater's location. Today, you can tour Shakespeare's Globe, watch a play performed there, or even take acting lessons there. As of 2015, the Globe Theatre released the Globe Player, which is the first ever play-on-demand website. On the website, you can download and watch the Globe's productions from anywhere in the world. Renting a Globe production costs about four pounds (about $5.75), while buying a download costs

The new Globe Theatre was built based on historical accounts and archaeological findings of the original theater, although it has certainly come into the twenty-first century.

eight pounds (about $11.50). There are even free videos available. Of particular interest is "Shakespeare Lives: *Twelfth Night*," which shows five UK artists creating new lyrics based on the Bard's play. The Globe Theatre has certainly come into the modern, digital age!

Many famous actors and actors have played in Shakespeare's *Twelfth Night*. Here, Judi Dench, as Maria, performs next to actors James Culliford, John Neville, and Derek Go.

it was many years before they were performed (again) as he had originally written them.

Today, of course, the plays are performed both in theaters and in films, sometimes in costumes of the period (ancient Rome for *Julius Caesar*, medieval England for *Henry V*), sometimes in modern dress (*Richard III* has recently been reset in England in the 1930s). *Twelfth Night*, in particular, has enjoyed many interpretations of Shakespeare's original performance directions. In a performance in Minneapolis, Minnesota, in 1984, the play was set in a carnival, with all characters being members of a circus troupe. The play has also been reimagined in a contemporary high school and as a musical, with the music of jazz great Duke Ellington.

Perhaps the most significant modern retellings of Shakespeare's plays come from the change of status of women since Elizabethan times. Today, women populate stage performances, although in 2002, the Globe Theatre's artistic director and well-known actor Mark Rylance played the role of Olivia in *Twelfth Night*. This was unusual; in most modern productions women now play the female characters. Many famous actresses have played either Olivia or Viola in *Twelfth Night*, including Diana Rigg, Judi Dench, Helena Bonham Carter, Helen Hunt, and Kyra Sedgwick.

Twelfth Night

The comedic play *Twelfth Night, or What You Will* was most likely written around 1601 for the Christmas season. "Twelfth Night" refers to the celebration on the twelfth day following Christmas, called Epiphany, when in the Christian tradition the three magi visited the baby Jesus. For the Twelfth Night feast during Shakespeare's time, it was common to bake a "king's cake" in which a bean was hidden. Whoever received the piece of cake with the bean would be considered the king for that day's celebrations. After midnight, the designated king would no longer rule. Celebrations focused on a reversal of what was considered normal for the time; thus, anyone, whether a pauper or a prince, could be crowned king for the day.

Shakespeare's *Twelfth Night* was written for these festivities. In this comedy, many roles are reversed, such as a woman, Viola, dressing as a man, and a servant, named Malvolio, acting as if he were a nobleman. Nothing is

Mark Rylance memorably played the role of Olivia in the 2013 Broadway revival of *Twelfth Night*.

as it seems in *Twelfth Night*, and the comedic aspect of the play arises from what happens when the characters attempt to sort out the confusion.

Twelfth Night was written at the end of the comedic period of Shakespeare's career. He had already written most of his great comedies, including *Much Ado About Nothing* and *As You Like It*. Following *Twelfth Night*, Shakespeare would begin writing his most famous tragedies, including *Hamlet*, before ending his writing career around 1613. Little record exists of the first performances of this play, and it was not met with enormous success, although Shakespeare was already a famous playwright at the time. Written during his mid-career, *Twelfth Night* features some of the Bard's greatest talents, including ingenious plot twists, colorful characters and dialogue, slapstick humor mixed with pathos, farcical scenes, and delicate romantic comedy.

Twelfth Night tells the story of Viola and her twin brother, Sebastian, whom she believes has been lost at sea following the sinking of their ship. Coming ashore to the island of Illyria, Viola disguises herself as a young man named Cesario and begins to work for Duke Orsino, a nobleman who is in love with a woman named Olivia. Duke Orsino uses Viola, disguised as Cesario, to profess his love for Olivia, but soon Olivia falls for Cesario. A complicated love triangle results until Sebastian comes ashore and further complicates matters when Olivia mistakes him for Cesario. Traditional gender roles are treated humorously, providing the basis for this unexpected comedy.

Over the years, *Twelfth Night* has become one of Shakespeare's most beloved comedies, even though

The king's cake was an integral part of Twelfth Night festivities in Elizabethan England.

it contains no single memorably pictorial moment as some of his other plays do—such as Bottom with the ass's head in *A Midsummer Night's Dream*, Hamlet holding Yorick's skull, Romeo at Juliet's balcony, Falstaff in the tavern, or Mark Antony at Caesar's funeral. Its famous lines are relatively few, and none of its characters have the miraculous eloquence and vitality of a Hamlet or a Cleopatra. Yet at least one noted Shakespeare critic, Stephen Booth, ranks *Twelfth Night* as Shakespeare's supreme achievement.

Even in Shakespeare's day, critics remarked on the similarity between *Twelfth Night* and his earlier comedy *The Comedy of Errors*. But in the earlier play, there were *two* sets of twins (all male!) to maximize the comic confusion. *Twelfth Night* is a far more mature and poetic work, peopled with much more interesting characters.

Chapter Two

The Play's the Thing

Shakespearean comedies often begin with a world in turmoil. An event has thrown the regular order of things into chaos, and the characters must deal with their newfound world. Often, but not always, Shakespearean comedies highlight the plight of two lovers who, due to societal restrictions, cannot be together. These characters flee, or are forced to flee, to a new land or society. In the case of *Twelfth Night*, a shipwreck is what exiles Viola and Sebastian from their homeland—the fictional country of Messaline. In the new land, these comedic characters disguise themselves as others, and the societal order is turned upside down. The resolution of these plays often has to do with the return of these characters, their acceptance in their society and/ or the acceptance of their love, and a wedding or other celebration. Shakespearian comedies, more than anything, explore the (happy) possibilities that are created when social order and strict family rules are bucked.

Twelfth Night has been performed for over four hundred years; this playbill dates to 1903.

VIOLA ALLEN

AS "VIOLA" IN SHAKESPEARE'S COMEDY

TWELFTH NIGHT

CHARLES W. ALLEN
MANAGER

Twelfth Night is a typical Shakespearean comedy in this sense. Twins Viola and Sebastian arrive in Illyria, although Viola mistakenly believes her brother has drowned. Highborn Viola disguises herself as a man named Cesario and turns around the social order when she works as a page for the lovesick Duke Orsino. The Duke is in love with Countess Olivia, and sends Viola as Cesario to deliver messages to the Countess. This sets up the conflict, and love triangle, that defines the rest of the play: Viola falls in love with the Duke, who is in love with Olivia. Olivia, believing Viola as Cesario to be a man, falls in love with her. In typical Shakespearian fashion, the conflict arises from Viola's disguise and her mistaken identity. Only when her identity is restored can this conflict be resolved.

Act I, Scene 1

Overview

The play begins in Duke Orsino of Illyria's palace. He is listening to music with his servant Curio while moodily expressing his unrequited love for the Countess Olivia. His first lines show his lovesickness and sadness without expressing why he feels this way: "If music be the food of love, play on: Give me excess of it, that, surfeiting, the appetite may sicken, and so die." Suddenly, Orsino tells the musician to stop playing, stating that it does not sound "so sweet now as it was before." When Curio inquires whether Orsino would like to go hunting, Orsino turns the conversation to his love for Olivia, stating "my desires [for her], like fell and cruel hounds, e'er since pursue me."

This engraving shows Duke, Curio, and musicians at the duke's palace at the opening of the play.

Then Valentine, another of Orsino's servants, enters the scene. Orsino had sent Valentine to call on Olivia for him, but Valentine has bad news. He says that, due to the recent death of Olivia's brother, she will not be accepting any visitors for seven years. This is how Olivia, in her grief, will keep her brother's memory alive. Although Orsino is disappointed that he will not see Olivia, he is impressed by the "debt of love" she holds for her brother. He reflects that, if Olivia is so steadfast in her love for her brother, then she will be even more faithful and loving when she falls in love with a man. Of course, Orsino hopes that this will be him.

Analysis

This brief scene introduces the motifs of love and music. We learn that Orsino and Olivia are both sentimentalists, given to extravagant emotions about love. As always, Shakespeare uses economical means to provide essential information for the audience and to create a distinctive emotional atmosphere for his story.

Act I, Scene 2

Overview

Viola, along with the sea captain and sailors, has reached the coast of Illyria after the ship she was traveling in with her brother sank. Talking with the captain, she expresses her fear that her brother Sebastian has drowned. However, the captain says that, while he doesn't know for sure if he has survived, he last saw Sebastian tied to the strong mast of the ship and holding "acquaintance with the waves." This gives Viola hope that her brother has survived the shipwreck after all.

Next, Viola asks the captain if he knows the land where they now find themselves. He says that he does, and he tells Viola about Orsino. She remembers that her father had mentioned his name and that he was unmarried back then. The captain states that he is still unmarried, although there is much gossip that he is in love with the fair Olivia. The captain explains that Olivia's father passed away a year earlier and that her brother died very recently. As readers already know from the first scene, Olivia has "abjured the company and sight of men" while she is grieving her brother. This impresses Viola, who states, "O that I served that lady and might not be delivered to the world, till I had made mine own occasion mellow." The captain reminds Viola, however, that Olivia will not allow anyone into her home.

Quickly, Viola comes up with a plan. She will disguise herself as a eunuch (a castrated man who usually aided a ruler) so that she can serve Orsino. She does not want to reveal her true identity until she becomes familiar with Illyria. Viola requests that the captain keep her secret and he vows, "Be you his eunuch, and your mute I'll be: when my tongue blabs, then let mine eyes not see." (This is the first and only time readers learn of Viola's plan to pose as a eunuch; she apparently abandons the idea later on.)

Analysis

Another brief scene sketches the situation for us. The brave Viola, one of Shakespeare's many twins surviving one of Shakespeare's many shipwrecks, forms her plan of action: disguising her sex (as many of Shakespeare's young women do), she will pose as a servant for Orsino.

As usual, the Bard shows his great skill in exposition, quickly and clearly providing the basic facts we need in order to follow a story that will soon become complex, as Viola, one of his most charming and ingenious heroines, mediates between Orsino and Olivia. Yet Viola's very first remark about the duke—she recalls that he used to be a bachelor—is a tip-off to how the play will end.

Like Olivia, Viola has (apparently) lost a brother. Unlike Olivia, however, she does not let her grief paralyze her. From the first moment she hears the name Orsino, she notes that he was unmarried when she last heard of him, and she quickly resolves to seek employment with him by disguising her sex. Already we sense her possible romantic interest in this eligible duke.

Act I, Scene 3

Overview

At Olivia's house, Sir Toby Belch, Olivia's uncle, is complaining about his niece's decision to mourn her brother in such a way. Sir Toby Belch is a loud, arrogant, and hard-drinking man, to whom Olivia often objects. Maria, Olivia's maid, attempts to tell Sir Toby that he is visiting too late and drinking too much. She tells Sir Toby that she overheard her lady talking about her dislike for his behavior, and especially of how she dislikes "a foolish knight that [Sir Toby] brought in one night here to be her wooer."

This foolish knight is Sir Andrew Aguecheek, a rich and very tall man who is also somewhat dimwitted. Sir Toby quickly defends Sir Andrew to Maria, and the audience might sense that Sir Toby's admiration of the

In Peter Hall's *Twelfth Night*, Sir Toby (Simon Callow),
Fabian (Samuel James), and Sir Andrew (Charles Edwards)
scheme against the hapless Malvolio (Simon Paisley Day).

knight is due solely to his wealth. As Sir Toby is defending him, Sir Andrew arrives. When Sir Toby introduces him to Maria, Sir Andrew makes several comic faux pas, such as misunderstanding Maria's name. Quickly, he is shown to be quite the fool. His exchange with Maria provokes great laughs from audiences; Maria jokes with him and calls him a fool to his face, although Sir Andrew does not understand. Although Sir Toby encourages Sir Andrew to stay and showers him with compliments, Sir Andrew is too dense to understand that Sir Toby, too, is mocking him. In one telling moment of self-analysis, Sir Andrew states, "Methinks sometimes I have no more wit than a Christian or an ordinary man has: but I am a great eater of beef and I believe that does harm to my wit." This shows that Sir Andrew is dimly aware of his lack of intelligence, all while further painting him as a fool.

Toward the end of the scene, Sir Andrew states that he will leave tomorrow because Olivia obviously does not want to see him. Sir Andrew even mentions that he has heard that the count himself hopes to woo Olivia. Sir Toby states that Sir Andrew still has a chance of being with Olivia because Olivia does not want anything to do with the count and will not marry anyone who is older or of a higher social class than her. This convinces Sir Andrew to stay for another month in the hopes that he will win over the fair Olivia. The two knights then plan a night of revelry, or partying, before the end of the scene.

Analysis

Here we enter the countess Olivia's house, where most of the play's central action takes place. Shakespeare gives us an intimate look at some of that household's wilder characters. We make the acquaintance of the playful Maria, the drunken Sir Toby, and the luckless Sir Andrew, three perpetrators of the play's great prank. (We have not yet met one of the chief characters, Malvolio, the target of their comic conspiracy.)

Act I, Scene 4

Overview

This scene opens in Orsino's palace, with Viola disguised as Cesario. Valentine remarks that he is impressed that Cesario has gained the duke's trust while working for him for just three days. Then Orsino arrives on the scene, telling Cesario that he has "unclasp'd to thee the book even of my secret soul," meaning that he has trusted Cesario with all of his secrets. He directs Cesario to go to Olivia and declare Orsino's love for her and not to leave until he is able to do so. Viola, as Cesario, however, is not so sure. She tells the duke that she doubts Olivia will receive her. To which Orsino replies, "Diana's lip is not more smooth and rubious; thy small pipe is as the maiden's organ, shrill and sound, and all is semblative a woman's part. I know thy constellation is right apt for this affair." In short, the duke states that Cesario is so young and delicate that he looks like a woman and that, because of his feminine airs, he is more likely to gain the trust of Olivia. In a secret aside to the audience, however, Viola expresses why she does not want to do this errand for the duke—she is in love with him herself! She states, "Whoe'er I woo, myself would be his wife!"

She's the Man

IN 2006, AMANDA Bynes, Channing Tatum, Laura Ramsey, and Vinnie Jones starred in a retelling of *Twelfth Night* called *She's the Man.*

Set in a modern American high school, Viola (played by Amanda Bynes) has only one desire: to play soccer on the high school team. Even though she is cut from the girls' team, she refuses to give up her dream. Instead, she disguises herself as her twin brother, Sebastian (played by James Kirk), in order to join the boys' team. Her successful disguise goes further, however. Soon, she becomes a student at an elite boys' prep school (named Illyria) by posing as her twin brother. There, she meets Duke Orsino (played by Channing Tatum), with whom she quickly falls in love.

She's the Man questions gender stereotypes—just like *Twelfth Night*—and attempts to show that Viola can succeed at anything she sets her mind to, despite the fact that the people around her don't believe in her capabilities when she's visibly a girl. The film doesn't follow Shakespeare's play too closely, however. Marriages do not end the film, but Viola and Orsino do get to share a special moment at the debutante ball. While Orsino does have feelings for a pretty Olivia, she is his lab partner, not a countess, and her story becomes less important. In fact, a major part of the play is not represented in the movie at all. There is no plot hatched by Maria to make a fool of Malvolio. Malvolio only makes one on-screen appearance—as a tarantula!

Although *She's the Man* didn't receive much critical acclaim, it is a fun retelling of *Twelfth Night* and one that most students might relate to a bit more than the Shakespearean play.

She's the Man was released around the world in 2006; this is the German poster for the film.

The famous English actress Ellen Alice Terry, dressed here as Viola, circa 1895

Analysis

The sweet and resourceful Viola shows herself equal to the challenges presented to her. She must handle delicate relations with both Orsino and Olivia, while concealing both her identity and her gender. In addition, she has her own passion to deal with: Can she win Orsino's heart? If she can, she may move all the way from the lowly position of page to duchess of Illyria—though it is really Orsino's heart that she craves, not the title. Yet it is notable, and entirely to Viola's credit, that she is absolutely loyal to Orsino, and she never even thinks of undermining his courtship of another woman—although, in her position, it would be easy for her to do so.

Act I, Scene 5

Overview

In Olivia's house, Maria is questioning Olivia's jester, Feste, about where he has been. Feste has been absent from Olivia's house for a long time, and Maria tells him that his mistress is not happy. The two exchange banter for some time, further displaying Maria's wit. Then Olivia enters the scene with her stern steward, Malvolio. Olivia directs Malvolio to remove Feste from her house, saying "Take the fool away." Feste playfully challenges Olivia, stating that he will prove that she is a fool, not him, and Olivia accepts the challenge. "Why mournest thou?" he asks his lady, to which she responds "for my brother's death." When Feste prods Olivia, she states that she knows her brother's soul is in heaven. To which Feste responds: "The more fool, madonna, to mourn for your brother's soul being in heaven. Take away the fool, gentlemen." Feste has proven his point, and Olivia is delighted by his wit.

Olivia turns to Malvolio, and asks him whether or not he is impressed with Feste. But the sour Malvolio states that Feste will become a better fool only once he is older and infirm. This piques Feste's interest, and he challenges Malvolio to prove that he is not a fool. But Malvolio will have none of it. Quickly, Olivia takes the side of her jester and insults the serious Malvolio, stating, "Oh, you are sick of self-love, Malvolio, and taste with a distempered appetite." Malvolio's "self-love" will soon become a point of jest for the other characters in the play.

Interrupting this conversation, Maria announces the arrival of a gentleman from Orsino's court. The audience knows that this is Viola, disguised as Cesario, come to declare the duke's love for Olivia. A half-drunk Sir Toby has been delaying Cesario from entering. Olivia orders Malvolio to get rid of the gentleman by telling him that she is sick or not at home. But soon Malvolio returns, stating that the gentleman (Cesario) will not take any of his excuses and insists on seeing Olivia. According to Malvolio, Cesario says that "he'll stand at [Olivia's] door like a sheriff's post ... but he'll speak with you." Finally, putting on a veil, Olivia agrees to go out and meet Orsino's page.

Viola, upon meeting Olivia, insists on speaking with her alone. Olivia sends away her servants and listens to what Viola, as Cesario, has to say. As we know, Viola professes the duke's love for Olivia, stating that Orsino loves Olivia "[w]ith adorations, fertile tears, with groans that thunder love, with sighs of fire." But Olivia remains firm; she does not love the duke and does not want to

Orsino and Viola by Frederick Richard Pickersgill

see him. Upon sending Viola away, Olivia tries to pay her, but Viola will not take her money. Viola departs.

Alone, Olivia admits that she has fallen for the duke's messenger. She states, "Methinks I feel this youth's perfections with an invisible and subtle stealth to creep in at mine eyes." Olivia's resolution to remain cloistered for seven years has been broken! She summons Malvolio and comes up with a plan to entice Viola to return, stating that the messenger has left his ring. Malvolio soon leaves to chase Viola and return the ring.

Analysis

This scene develops one of the play's central themes: the confusion of the sexes that will provide so much of the fun (as well as seriousness). We meet the grumpy steward Malvolio, whom it is so tempting to dislike, in spite of the very real virtues Olivia esteems in him. He is not, after all, an evil man; on the contrary, he is honest and trustworthy, and he harms nobody. Even his enemies recognize that he is virtuous, even if, like most of Shakespeare's villains, he doesn't know how to have fun. Malvolio reminds us that virtue is not always amiable. Can he be blamed if Olivia delegates to him the tasks she prefers not to do herself? We resent him merely for doing his duty.

We are not told how long Malvolio has been a steward. He does not seem new to the position; was he employed by Olivia's father and brother too? We can only guess. Olivia certainly has high regard for him, though she is quick to scold him when she thinks it appropriate.

It may also be worth bearing in mind that Olivia lost both her father and her brother only recently, so she has not held her estate for very long. Yet she rules it with intelligence and authority, and she is determined not to let her dissolute uncle, Sir Toby, take advantage of her.

Illyria is still part of the feudal world, where most people keep the status they were born with and social mobility is very limited. This is why Malvolio's secret ambition to marry Olivia is so comical. Olivia herself puts her finger on his weakness: self-love. With a little nudge, Malvolio will be revealed as the social climber he secretly is.

Act II, Scene 1

Overview

Act II begins at the sea coast of Illyria, where Sebastian is revealed to have survived the shipwreck. Speaking with another sea captain, Antonio, Sebastian reveals his identity and expresses his belief that his sister Viola has drowned. Sebastian, in his grief, praises his sister for her beauty and her mind and, seduced by Sebastian's sadness, Antonio resolves to be his servant. Sebastian denies him, saying that he will go alone to Orsino's court. But Antonio, who "adores [Sebastian] so," follows him, although he admits that he has enemies in the duke's court and that it could be dangerous for him to go there.

Analysis

This brief scene confirms that Viola's twin brother has survived the shipwreck. Like Viola, Sebastian inspires affection, even devotion. Antonio is already willing to risk his own life to help his handsome and charming young friend who believes his lovely sister has drowned.

Antonio's love for Sebastian adds one more strand to what is becoming a complex plot.

In fact, some critics rank the plot of *Twelfth Night* as Shakespeare's most ingenious. Though it has no fairies, witches, oracles, or other supernatural elements, it does contain devices found in many of the Bard's other comedies: a shipwreck, separated twins, and a heroine in masculine disguise. These are ancient stage conventions, and it matters very little whether or not they are actually plausible.

Shakespeare's artistry and mastery of drama are evident in the way he shows us so early that Sebastian has survived the shipwreck. If Shakespeare had delayed this revelation until late in the play, it would seem to us an implausible coincidence. By telling us at the beginning of the second act and frequently reminding us of it, he prepares us for later story developments that we might otherwise find hard to accept.

Act II, Scene 2

Overview

Malvolio has caught up with Viola, asking if it was she who had just visited Olivia. Giving her the ring, Malvolio once again states that Olivia is not interested in Orsino and never will be. When she will not take the ring, Malvolio throws it down on the street and says that Viola can take it if she wants it.

Once Malvolio leaves, Viola expresses her confusion. Obviously, she had not left a ring with Olivia and wonders why she made up this story. Soon, Viola reaches a plausible conclusion: Olivia, believing Viola to be a man, is in love with her! This scene introduces the tangled web of desires

This portrait shows actor William Pleater Davidge (1814–1888) in the role of Malvolio.

that provides the basis for the play: Viola loves Orsino, who loves Olivia, who loves Viola. And more confused desires will add up throughout the rest of the play.

Analysis

Poor Viola, in love with her master Orsino, now finds that the great lady he has sent her to woo has fallen in love with her in her male disguise! She is becoming more and more keenly aware of the curious position she occupies—she even calls herself a "monster" who belongs to both sexes at once. She sums up her own plight in a soliloquy:

> *What will become of this? As I am man,*
> *My state is desperate for my master's love;*
> *As I am woman (now alas the day!),*
> *What thriftless sighs shall poor Olivia breathe!*
> *O time, thou must untangle this, not I,*
> *It is too hard a knot for me t'untie.*

Act II, Scene 3

Overview

Sir Toby and Sir Andrew, both drunk, are enjoying a late night of drink and revelry at Olivia's house. Feste soon joins them, and the three joke and sing together until their noisy revelry wakes up Maria. She comes in to scold them, stating that Olivia will send Malvolio to throw them out if they wake her. But the three men do not care and continue their boisterous jokes while Maria pleads with them to remain quiet.

Sure enough, Malvolio soon appears. He furiously scolds the revelers, asking them, "Have ye no wit, manners, nor honesty, but to gabble like tinkers at this time of

Kulvinder Ghir, as Feste, takes the stage in an adaptation of *Twelfth Night* set in India.

night?" When Sir Toby continues to joke, the angry steward singles Toby out for a special rebuke as Olivia's kinsman, threatening to expel him unless he mends his rowdy ways. This fails to quell the knight's insolence. He and Feste sing snatches of a ballad mocking Malvolio, and Sir Toby asks the haughty steward, in a famous sarcasm, "Dost thou think, because thou art virtuous, there shall be no more cakes and ale?" Then Sir Toby orders Maria to bring him some wine. As she obeys, Malvolio says he will report her to Olivia, and he departs in a fury.

Led by Maria, the incensed revelers agree on a plot against Malvolio. Maria says she can fake Olivia's handwriting well enough to fool Olivia herself, so she proposes to forge a love letter to Malvolio, causing him to think Olivia is in love with him and inviting him to woo her. Delighted with the prank, they part. Sir Toby, remarking that it is too late to go to bed now, tells Sir Andrew to get more money. It is finally dawning on Sir Andrew that he may not win Olivia's hand, but the greedy Sir Toby keeps giving him false encouragement.

Analysis

The full impact of this rowdy scene is hard to figure out from reading it on the page. Sir Toby, Sir Andrew, and Feste are carousing when Maria comes to caution them that they will arouse Malvolio, but she soon joins in the fun herself, just as Malvolio makes his appearance. They then begin to hatch a plot to humiliate Malvolio, in an effort to break his seriousness and apparent narcissism. This sets up the second-most important plot of the play, after the love triangle between the three main characters. Malvolio signifies societal order and an unwillingness to celebrate the Twelfth Night festivities. Considered the antagonist of this comedic play, Malvolio will be ruthlessly mocked right up until the end.

Act II, Scene 4

Overview

Back at the duke's palace, Orsino tells Cesario (Viola) that he would like to listen to "the old and antique" song that he heard the night before. Curio tells Orsino that Feste should sing the song, because he knows it well, but that Feste is not there. Orsino sends Curio out to bring Feste in, then signals the musicians to begin playing. Turning to Cesario, Orsino asks, "How dost thou like this tune?" Cesario eloquently praises it. Then, ever the romantic, Orsino asks Cesario if he has ever been in love before. Cesario answers in the affirmative. What kind of woman is't?" the duke asks. "Of your complexion," Cesario responds. Next, Orsino asks the age of the woman with whom Cesario fell in love. "About your years, my lord," Cesario responds. While Orsino states that the woman did not seem to be a good fit for Cesario, the audience knows that Cesario is actually speaking about the duke himself.

Soon, Curio arrives with Feste. To please the duke, Feste begins to sing the song from the other night. It is a sad song, and includes some of the Bard's most famous lyrics: "Come away, come away, death, and in sad cypress let me be laid; fly away, fly away breath; I am slain by a fair cruel maid." At the end of the song, Orsino tries to pay Feste for his time, but Feste refuses the money and leaves.

After the entertainment is over, the duke is once again alone with Cesario. Once again, he asks Cesario

Bridget Flanery, as Viola, and Geoffrey Lower, as Orsino, banter in this production of *Twelfth Night* performed in Pershing Square, Los Angeles.

to declare the duke's undying love to Olivia. "But if she cannot love you, sir?" Cesario responds. The duke answers that he cannot accept that response, but Cesario states that he must. Again, Viola, disguised as Cesario, secretly declares her own love for the duke, saying, "Say that some lady, as perhaps there is, hath for your love as great a pang of heart as you have for Olivia." Viola continues her wise words to the duke, saying that the woman who loves the duke might herself have to admit the fact that the duke does not love her, just as the duke has to accept his unrequited love for Olivia. But the duke refuses to believe that a woman could love him as much as he loves Olivia. He states that "no woman's heart [is so] big, to hold so much [love]." Viola, of course, disagrees. She says that her own father had a daughter who loved a man but never revealed her love and instead pined away silently for him—and this proves that women love more deeply than men. Of course Viola is secretly talking about herself and Orsino, but he misses her hidden meaning. He hands her a jewel to take to Olivia with the message that his love can endure no refusal.

Analysis

Viola's plight is dramatized in this scene. As Cesario, she is bound to serve and obey Orsino, even when he commands her to help him woo Olivia. She is careful to speak ambiguously, often telling Orsino the truth so ingeniously that he fails to recognize her real meaning. Her position is both awkward and painful, and her selfless behavior—doing her best to help Orsino win Olivia's hand—commands both our respect and our sympathy.

Act II, Scene 5

Overview

In Olivia's garden, Sir Toby, Sir Andrew, and Fabian (a member of the household) look forward gleefully to the prank on Malvolio. Maria comes to alert them that Malvolio is on his way. She leaves; the others all hide as he enters, talking to himself.

As it happens, Malvolio at that moment is daydreaming aloud of marrying Olivia. He recalls that Maria once claimed Olivia liked him, and at another time Olivia herself told him that if she were attracted to a man, it would be to someone who looked like Malvolio. This is enough to amuse the three pranksters greatly as they eavesdrop on his soliloquy; they can barely keep quiet. Sir Toby nearly explodes in anger and laughter when Malvolio imagines himself a man of high rank: "Count Malvolio!" (We must remember that a steward was, after all, a mere servant.) The reverie goes on, as Malvolio imagines himself Olivia's husband, loftily ordering his servants to summon "my kinsman Toby" and Toby obediently curtseying to him. Overhearing all this, Sir Toby is nearly beside himself with fury at the steward's presumption. It gets no better when Malvolio pictures himself ordering "Cousin Toby" to "amend your drunkenness" and cease wasting time with a "foolish knight." (Sir Andrew, shrewd as ever, recognizes himself in this description: "I knew 'twas I, for many do call me fool.")

Just then Malvolio sees the forged letter. He picks it up and thinks he recognizes Olivia's handwriting. He reads it eagerly and takes the bait exactly as the pranksters have hoped. He also thinks he recognizes the letter's phrasing as Olivia's. The whole thing seems to refer to him in a code he has no trouble interpreting. "Some are born great," the letter says, "some achieve greatness, and some have greatness thrust upon 'em." It goes on to urge Malvolio to dress absurdly in yellow stockings, cross-gartered, and not to resist his good fortune unless he wants to remain a mere steward, stuck with the other servants all his life.

Malvolio is ecstatic, exulting that "my lady loves me!" The letter's meaning is undeniable. Then he notices the postscript. It urges him to smile if he welcomes her (presumably Olivia's) love. The sour-faced Malvolio, now enraptured with hopes, promises to smile constantly.

When Malvolio has gone, Sir Toby, Sir Andrew, and Fabian roar with delight at Maria's inspired trick, so perfectly put into practice. They congratulate her as she reappears at that moment. She invites them to

Malvolio arrives in his cross garters, to the delight of Maria, Sir Toby Belch, and Fabian.

The Play's the Thing   **49**

watch the rest of the prank as Malvolio greets Olivia in his new garb—which she is sure to hate, for she dislikes yellow stockings, loathes cross-gartering, and, being in mourning for her brother, will be in no mood for her steward's excessive smiling.

Analysis

The hoax not only succeeds brilliantly, but also exposes Malvolio's secret nature: besides hiding a huge ego under his very proper exterior, he has a romantic heart that longs not just for power and status, but simply for love. In a way, this exposure of normal human weakness under an icy exterior will be Malvolio's deepest humiliation of all, since he pretends to be better than everyone else. It also makes Malvolio much more sympathetic to the audience.

Act III, Scene 1

Overview

Still in Olivia's garden, Viola/Cesario banters with Feste, who says he is not Olivia's fool, since she has no folly, but is instead her "corrupter of words." Despite their duel of wits, their mutual respect is clear. As Feste departs, leaving Viola alone, she muses that this apparent fool is indeed a wise man. Even feigning folly, she reflects, requires "a kind of wit."

Sir Toby and Sir Andrew arrive, and Sir Toby invites Viola into Olivia's house just as Olivia and Maria enter. Olivia requests that everyone leave, so that she can speak to Viola, who she believes to be Cesario, alone. Again, Viola attempts to speak of the duke's love for Olivia, but Olivia wants none of it. Olivia states, "O, by your leave,

I pray you, I bade you never speak again of him: but, would you undertake another suit, I had rather hear you to solicit that than music from the spheres." Here, Olivia is dangerously close to admitting to Viola/Cesario her feelings. She states that she no longer wants to hear about Orsino's love for her, but, if Cesario came to speak to her of something else, she would rather listen to Cesario than "music from the spheres."

Before Viola/Cesario can speak, Olivia interrupts her. She admits that the ring was a ruse for Cesario to return. What must Cesario think of her? Olivia wonders this aloud. She continues to hint at her true feelings: "a cypress, not a bosom, hideth my heart." When Olivia begs Cesario to speak, however, Cesario responds, "I pity you." Excited, Olivia states that pity is a form of love. No, Viola as Cesario responds, because we can often pity our enemies as well.

Soon, Olivia begins to speak more directly. She asks Cesario what he thinks of her. A somewhat confusing exchange occurs, with both characters agreeing that they are not what the other thinks they are. Of course, this refers to Cesario being a woman (Viola) in disguise, and the countess Olivia falling in love with Orsino's page.

Finally, Olivia admits what is on her mind: "Cesario, by the roses of the spring, by maidhood, honour, truth and every thing, I love thee so, that, maugre all thy pride, Nor wit nor reason can my passion hide." Viola/Cesario, who suspected this, swears on her life that no woman has ever held her heart. Of course, this is literally true while also keeping her true gender concealed. Viola bids Olivia "adieu" and promises that she will never come back to express her master's love. But, before she leaves, Olivia bids Cesario to come again to express the duke's love so that Olivia may see her love again.

Analysis

This scene deepens the play's themes of the nature of the sexes and the contrast between wit and folly. In Shakespeare's day, the word "wit" had a broader set of meanings than it has now. It included not only humor and cleverness, but also intelligence, reasoning ability, sanity, insight, and wisdom. (The term "halfwit" is now used only as an insult, but it used to describe a person who was mentally disabled. It was not considered offensive.)

The clown Feste and the disguised Viola engage in the wordplay so typical of Shakespeare, especially in this play, which abounds in puns, silly logic, mock scholarship, and other amusing verbal devices. Feste, who describes himself as a "corrupter of words," remarks that "words are grown so false, I am loath to prove reason with them."

Alone with Olivia a few moments later, Viola still makes a game of speaking in riddles, telling the lady that "you do think you are not what you are" and "I am not what I am." These hints of Viola's disguise, of course, go over Olivia's head. When Olivia's love for Cesario is unrequited, she finds herself in the same position as Orsino, whose love she has scorned.

Act III, Scene 2

Overview

Realizing that he cannot gain Olivia's heart, Sir Andrew promises that he will leave Olivia's house right away. When asked why, Sir Andrew states that he saw Olivia bestowing "more favours" to Cesario than to him. Fabian

Sir Toby (*center*) mischievously attempts to convince Sir Andrew to duel with Cesario/Viola.

tries to convince Sir Andrew that Olivia did this just to make Sir Andrew jealous. Suspicious, Sir Andrew inquires: "[W]ill you make an ass o' me?" Of course, this will be the beginning of another scheme to make Sir Andrew look foolish. Sir Toby picks up on Fabian's scheme and states that Sir Andrew is missing his opportunity by not actively pursuing Olivia. He states that Sir Andrew should show his valor by challenging Cesario to a duel. They succeed in convincing Sir Andrew to write a letter to Cesario immediately, and Sir Andrew rushes off to do so.

After Sir Andrew leaves, Fabian and Sir Toby laugh about their plot, agreeing that both Cesario and Sir Andrew will be too cowardly to fight. Then, Maria arrives with news about their other plot. Malvolio has dressed himself outlandishly in yellow stockings and cross garters to prove his love for Olivia according to the forged letter.

Maria states that she had never seen Malvolio looking so foolish, and the three rush off to see the spectacle.

Analysis

This scene advances the plot in two respects. First, we learn that Sir Andrew is realizing—better late than never—that he is wasting his time trying to win Olivia's favor; she obviously prefers Cesario. In order to prevent Sir Andrew from leaving, Sir Toby urges him to impress Olivia with his valor by challenging Cesario to a duel, which Sir Toby assumes that both men will be afraid to fight. This prepares us for a surprise when the scheme goes wrong. Sir Andrew goes off to write a challenge.

Second, we learn that Malvolio has been completely taken in by Maria's forged letter. The hoax has been a triumph. Three men now aspire to marry Olivia—Orsino, Sir Andrew, and Malvolio. But they are all destined to fail, for she loves only Cesario—who, of course, can never marry her.

Act III, Scene 3

Overview

Viola's twin brother, Sebastian, is approaching Orsino's estate with the sea captain Antonio. Sebastian thanks Antonio for accompanying him and asks Antonio if he wants to see the sights of the city. But Antonio says that he is in great danger walking around the city streets. Antonio alludes to the fact that once, in a sea-fight, he looted from Orsino's men. Preferring to hide himself, Antonio gives Sebastian money and proposes that they meet at the Elephant Inn. The two leave one another with the promise to rejoin each other's company later that night.

Analysis

In this scene, the Bard lays the groundwork for several dramatic turns: the reunion of the twins, the duel between Sir Andrew and Cesario, and, most unexpectedly, the sudden marriage of Olivia, in spite of her vow to remain single for seven years in mourning for her brother.

Sebastian's survival from the shipwreck could have been a loose end in the plot of the play, but Shakespeare ingeniously builds a whole subplot on it, so that it strikes us as almost inevitable rather than arbitrary.

Act III, Scene 4

Overview

At the beginning of this long scene in Olivia's garden, Olivia tells Maria that she has sent a request to Cesario to come back. She frets over what to do when he arrives. Then, she asks Maria where Malvolio is. She would like to see her "sad and civil" servant because she is feeling morose and would enjoy his company. Here, Maria plays up her plot. Malvolio is coming, she says, but he is acting very strangely. Maria suggests that he might even be possessed and states that he does nothing but smile as if he were mad. Olivia directs Maria to bring him to her.

When Maria returns with Malvolio, the steward is indeed behaving strangely. He will not stop smiling, although Olivia says that she has sent for him during a "sad occasion." He is wearing his yellow stockings and garters and, hilariously, states, "I could be sad: this does

The comic climax of the play occurs when Malvolio arrives in yellow stockings and cross garters, smiling stupidly, as shown in this 1891 engraving.

make some obstruction in the blood, this cross-gartering; but what of that?" As he speaks to Olivia, he alludes to his romantic feelings for her, hoping for her confirmation. Of course, Olivia doesn't know why he is acting in this strange way. Malvolio kisses Olivia's hand and compliments her; baffled, Olivia asks if he is feeling well and suggests he should go to bed. Undaunted, Malvolio begins to quote from the forged letter, further baffling Olivia. She states that Malvolio's strange behavior is "midsummer madness."

A servant announces the arrival of Orsino's young gentleman (Viola/Cesario). Olivia says she will go to him, but first she orders Maria to take care of Malvolio and make sure her people, including Sir Toby, see that no harm comes to him.

Malvolio, naturally, misconstrues Olivia's concern and thinks she is simply following her own prescriptions in the letter. He is flattered that no less a man than Sir Toby is (as he imagines) being put at his disposal. When Sir Toby, Fabian, and Maria enter, appealing to him to resist the devil that possesses him, he takes it all the wrong way and insults them ("You are idle shallow things; I am not of your element"). He tells them to go hang themselves as he rushes out in a rage.

The three pranksters savor their victory over the steward, and Sir Toby proposes that Malvolio be treated as a madman—bound and confined in a dark room for the time being, since Olivia already believes that he has lost his wits.

Sir Andrew rushes in excitedly, eager to show the others the challenge he has written to Cesario. Sir Toby, vastly amused at the success of this new trick, pretends to approve of the foolish knight's boldness and encourages him to keep it up. When Sir Andrew is gone, he says he will not deliver the letter to young Cesario, but instead will report to Cesario that the knight is in a terrible fury. When he is finished with them, both of the prospective combatants will be far too frightened of each other to have a duel.

Olivia and Cesario enter, and the others depart. Olivia gives Cesario a jewel with her picture in it and beseeches the "servant" to come again the next day. Viola/Cesario accepts this gift as tactfully as she can, for her master's sake. Olivia exits.

Sir Toby and Fabian enter. They warn Cesario that Sir Andrew is a dreadful and furious adversary. Cesario protests that "he" has done nothing, as far as "he" knows, to offend anyone. Sir Toby answers that this does not matter; the brawling knight has already killed three men, and only more deaths will satisfy his present wrath.

"I am no fighter," Cesario objects, hoping that Olivia can afford "him" some protection. But Sir Toby continues to make Sir Andrew sound formidable, as does Fabian when Sir Toby leaves: "He is indeed, sir, the most skillful, bloody, and fatal opposite that you could possibly have found in any part of Illyria." Still, Fabian promises to make peace with Sir Andrew if he can.

As Fabian exits with the frightened Cesario, Sir Toby comes back with the equally frightened Sir Andrew, who says that if his enemy will abandon the duel he may have Sir Andrew's horse, Capilet. Cesario and Fabian return; Cesario and Sir Andrew, both goaded by Sir Toby (who assures each that there is really nothing to be afraid of), draw their swords on each other.

Now Antonio arrives looking for Sebastian! Mistaking Viola for her twin brother, he tells Sir Andrew to put up his sword, or he will fight for his young friend. Sir Toby also draws his sword, just as a group of officers comes to arrest Antonio on Orsino's behalf. Now Antonio is angry with Viola, who he thinks has been ungrateful for Antonio's kindnesses (the money he lent Sebastian, for instance).

When Antonio heatedly addresses Viola as Sebastian, her heart beats faster. Can this mean that her dear Sebastian has not drowned, but is still alive after all? It seems too good to be true! As Cesario exits, Sir Andrew is encouraged by the "boy's" display of cowardice and renews his challenge to a duel.

Analysis

This long scene is full of comic misunderstandings. Malvolio has been misled by the fake letter; his behavior baffles Olivia, who knows nothing of the letter he supposes she wrote. She thinks he has gone mad. Maria, the letter's real author, is amused by all of this and stays silent about the prank.

"If this were played upon a stage now, I could condemn it as an improbable fiction," says Fabian of the prank on Malvolio. This is Shakespeare's comment on his own play. It *is* being acted on the stage, and it *is* an improbable fiction. This remark serves to express, in a humorous way, the audience's feelings about the unrealistic nature of the theater. We may be reminded of Theseus's wise words in *A Midsummer Night's Dream*: "The best in this kind are but shadows"—that is, even the best plays are only make-believe.

Act IV, Scene 1

In front of Olivia's house, Sebastian is trying to get rid of Feste. Mistaking Sebastian for Cesario, Feste has followed Sebastian in order to bring him back to Olivia. Feste sarcastically states, "No, I do not know you; nor I am not sent to you by my lady, to bid you come speak with her; nor your name is not Master Cesario; nor this is not my nose neither. Nothing that is so is so." Feste is unaware of the truth that he speaks. Finally, Sebastian pays the fool to leave and offers to give him "worse payment," most likely a physical punishment, if he does not obey.

Sir Andrew now appears, with Sir Toby and Fabian. He mistakes Sebastian for the timid Cesario and gives him a blow, which Sebastian instantly gives him back, with the question, "Are all the people mad?" Sir Toby seizes Sebastian. Feste says he will report all of them to Olivia, and she will punish them. As Sebastian frees himself from Sir Toby's grip, the two men draw their swords.

Olivia enters and furiously orders her uncle to desist; she rebukes him for his extremely bad manners and apologizes to Sebastian. Overwhelmed by Olivia's sweet welcome, Sebastian thinks he must be dreaming. Olivia has mistaken Sebastian for Cesario. She asks him to go with her to her house. He is startled, but he gladly agrees.

Analysis

The play moves boisterously toward its conclusion, when all these misunderstandings will be corrected. As yet,

For his devotion to Olivia and his susceptibility to the ruse against him, Malvolio is told he is a madman and forcibly enclosed in a dark room.

nobody knows that Cesario is a girl, let alone that she has a twin brother. One way or another, nearly everyone but Viola is deceived by appearances. Feste's joke that "Nothing that is so is so" is an ironic statement that only the audience knows to be true.

Act IV, Scene 2

Overview

Outside the room where Malvolio has been confined, Maria impishly tells Feste to visit Malvolio disguised as Sir Topas, a priest. She gives Feste a gown and false beard to wear as she goes to bring Sir Toby. Feste agrees to go along with Maria's idea, but, alone, he is a little reluctant to take the prank so far. He puts on the gown and beard as Maria returns with Sir Toby, and he calls to Malvolio, identifying himself in a disguised voice as "Sir Topas the curate, who comes to visit Malvolio the lunatic." Malvolio insists that he is quite sane, but Feste keeps pulling his leg, playfully getting Malvolio into a foolish debate about Pythagoras and the doctrine of the reincarnation of the soul.

Sir Toby urges Feste to resume his natural voice. He thinks the prank on Malvolio has gone far enough—maybe a little too far, for it now risks making Olivia (who has high regard for her steward) angry. Now Feste sings to Malvolio in his own voice, but also speaks as Sir Topas, so that Malvolio thinks he is dealing with two separate men. Promising Feste a generous reward, Malvolio begs him for ink, paper, and light, so that he may prove his sanity to his lady.

In the final deception of the play, Feste impersonates a priest, under the name of Sir Topas, for the purpose of further befuddling Malvolio in his madman's cell. Malvolio thinks the clergyman will help him to get fair treatment, never suspecting that "Sir Topas" is merely a new addition to the conspiracy against him.

Act IV, Scene 3

Overview

Alone in Olivia's orchard, Sebastian is marveling at a pearl she has given him. He keeps repeating that what he is experiencing in the strange land of Illyria cannot be madness. But, he worries, where is his dear friend Antonio, who was supposed to meet him yesterday at the Elephant Inn? As Sebastian, who finds Olivia wholly admirable, tries to make some sense of the situation, Olivia arrives with a priest. She wants to marry Sebastian (whom she thinks is Cesario) in her chapel immediately. Sebastian happily agrees.

Analysis

In this short scene, a major part of the plot is resolved: Olivia's passion for Cesario is satisfied by her marriage to Viola's twin brother Sebastian.

Shakespeare ends one of his most joyous plays with unexpected marital pairings, beginning with this one. Though these unions are more fantastic than realistic, we forgive their improbability because they are so romantic, entertaining, and dramatically apt. As Fabian has said earlier of the prank on Malvolio, "If this were played upon a stage now, I could condemn it as an improbable fiction." The Bard is well aware of how unlikely his whole story is, with its shipwreck, separated twins, mistaken identities, playful conspiracy, lucky love triangle, and coincidences. One of his characters comments on this so that members of the audience will not feel they are being asked to accept too much.

Act V, Scene 1

Overview

At Olivia's estate, Feste has Malvolio's letter to Olivia. Fabian wants to read it, but the fool refuses to let him, for it proves that Malvolio is perfectly sane and has been confined wrongly.

Orsino arrives with Viola, Curio, and some lords. After some of his typical banter, Feste leaves. Several officers bring Antonio in, under arrest, and Viola recognizes him as the man who saved her (in her Cesario guise) from Sir Andrew.

Meanwhile, Antonio is angry at Viola, as he mistakes her for her twin brother, Sebastian, who appears to have betrayed him.

Olivia enters with her attendants. She of course mistakes Viola for Cesario, and accuses Cesario of betraying her when "he" denies that he is her husband. Orsino blames Viola/Cesario for stealing the heart of Olivia, still the object of his love, and Olivia summons the priest to attest that she is betrothed to the young man. The priest says that this is so.

Orsino becomes furious at Cesario, the "dissembling cub" whom he paid to help him court Olivia, but who

Actors (*from left to right*) Liam Brennan, Samuel Barnett, Joseph Timms, and Mark Rylance perform in the 2013 Broadway production of *Twelfth Night*.

betrayed him. Viola/Cesario tries to protest, but Sir Andrew arrives, calling for a surgeon for himself and Sir Toby. Both have been roughed up, it seems, by Cesario, but again Viola pleads innocent.

Now Sir Toby limps in, accompanied by Feste, complaining of his injury. As Sir Toby departs with Sir Andrew, Feste, and Fabian, Sebastian arrives and apologizes to Olivia for attacking her kinsman. Everyone is startled to see that he looks just like Cesario. Orsino and Antonio marvel at the resemblance first; then the twins themselves joyfully realize what has happened, and the whole company begins to comprehend. When Orsino sees that Cesario is actually a girl, his anger ceases, and his fondness for his page turns into romantic love.

Feste enters with Fabian, and Olivia orders him to read Malvolio's letter aloud. He begins to do so, but in such a ridiculously unnatural voice that she orders Fabian to read it instead. The letter convinces Olivia that there is nothing wrong with her steward's mind, and she directs Fabian to release him from the cell. When Malvolio comes forth, he accuses Olivia of having done him "notorious wrong," then shows her the letter he thought she had written to him.

Olivia admits that it is a good imitation of her own penmanship, but says it is undoubtedly Maria's writing. She sees how the practical joke was born, and she promises the angry steward full redress of the wrongs he has suffered. Fabian owns up to his part in the plot, but he says Malvolio brought it on himself with his malicious speech; he also mentions that Sir Toby has married Maria in "recompense" for her role in the prank.

Feste chimes in by reminding Malvolio of his earlier taunts and quoting passages from Maria's forgery. The humiliated steward goes out with a final threat: "I'll be revenged on the whole pack of you!" Olivia and Orsino take pity on him, and they send people to pacify him. Feste is left alone, and he concludes the play with a song.

Analysis

The play begins with music and unrequited love, and it ends with music and love fulfilled. Only one character— Malvolio—is excluded from the final festivities. In reality he excludes *himself* with his sour nature, which has made him an enemy of joy all along. Yet Shakespeare does not paint Malvolio as an evil man. True evil and malice can hardly exist in the enchanted world of *Twelfth Night*.

List of Characters

- Orsino, duke of Illyria
- Valentine and Curio, gentlemen attending Orsino

- Sir Toby Belch, uncle of Olivia
- Sir Andrew Aguecheek, companion of Sir Toby, suitor of Olivia
- Malvolio, Olivia's steward
- Fabian, Olivia's servant
- Feste, Olivia's jester
- Sebastian, Viola's twin brother
- Antonio, Sebastian's friend
- Sea Captain, Priest, Officers, Musicians, Servants
- Olivia, a rich countess
- Viola/Cesario, Sebastian's twin sister
- Maria, Olivia's gentlewoman

Analysis of Major Characters

Viola

Of all Shakespeare's heroines, Viola is one of the best loved. She is sweet, pure, loyal, quick-witted, and resourceful. Though she is cunning, she has no trace of cynicism, selfishness, or malice. Like all the Bard's finest creations, she is impossible to describe adequately. Her personality is so specific and lively that it must be known directly, not at second hand.

Viola, unlike other heroines, does not have a fatal flaw that will lead her to trouble. Ironically, while she is the character who spends nearly the entire plot in disguise, she is the purest. Viola's love for Orsino never wavers. This is contrary to the other characters in the play, who all waver in their affections throughout the plot; most notably Orsino, who will marry Viola at the end of the play, is not as steadfast in his love for Olivia as he initially declares. It is Viola's purity, steadfastness, and will that allows her to get what she truly desires—Orsino's love—thus ending the play.

Though she disguises herself as a young man for innocent reasons, Viola comes to regard disguise as "a wickedness" that plays into the devil's hands. Yet only in her first scene does the audience see her dressed as a woman. Of course, in Shakespeare's day, all theatrical characters were played by males (usually boys). This would have made Viola's progression even more ironic—and comedic—to an Elizabethan audience.

Finally, Viola could perhaps be viewed today as a feminist heroine. She is one of the wittiest characters in the play, and it is largely her action that directs the course of the plot. *Twelfth Night* revolves around Viola's actions, which are largely unimpeded when she is disguised as Cesario. At the end of the play, Viola sheds her disguise and is able to live freely as herself. However, Viola never does change into her female clothes. This has led some scholars to say that Shakespeare continued to play with gender roles, through the character of Viola, right up until the comedic end of the play.

Modern audiences can only marvel that Shakespeare wrote so many great female roles in both tragedy and comedy, given the status of women in Elizabethan England and the lack of women in the theater of his time. Even today, these roles challenge some of the greatest actresses in the world.

Orsino

At the beginning of the play, Orsino is called a duke, but later in the play, for some reason, he is referred to by the lesser title of count. He is a sentimental man

Olivia unveils herself to Cesario in
William Powell Frith's 1874 painting.

whose professions of love for Olivia are too shallow to mean very much. When he learns that she has married Sebastian and that the supposed boy Cesario is really the girl Viola, he quickly transfers his affection to Viola. This being a comedy, we have to assume that they live happily ever after, no matter how unworthy of Viola he may seem to us.

While Viola is steadfast and controlled in her love for Orsino, Orsino is exactly the opposite. He cannot control his love for Olivia; in fact, it is his romantic sentiments that seem to control him. While all ends well for Orsino, Shakespeare is certainly critiquing this character for his unbridled emotions. But balance is restored at the end of the play. Orsino gains balance from the character of Viola, who loves him thoughtfully and will tame his romanticism.

Olivia

The first thing we learn of the countess Olivia is that she has made a rather extreme decision to mourn her dead brother for seven years, during which time she will let no man see her. While this makes Olivia a very sympathetic character, it also sets her up to be a character, like Orsino, who is controlled by her emotions. Of course, Olivia does not remain steadfast in this decision. Upon meeting Cesario, she instantly forgets her pledge. (In the plays of Shakespeare, such vows are made to be broken.)

Just as Viola and her twin brother Sebastian are grouped together as almost interchangeable in some ways, so, too, are Olivia and Orsino incredibly similar. Orsino pines for someone who is just like him, but Olivia will have none of it. As Viola balances out Orsino, Sebastian will balance out Olivia.

As the mistress of her house, Olivia is very capable. She banters with her charges and treats them well. Olivia also relies on her capable steward Malvolio to enforce her orders and is always fair and kind with him, despite the fact that most of the other characters dislike him. If Olivia's flaw is that she can be moody and excessive, she is a kind character who does not wrong anyone throughout the course of the play.

Malvolio

The ill-tempered steward Malvolio, a born enemy of every kind of festivity, is the victim of a brilliant hoax, perfectly calculated to appeal to his secret vanity and to expose it for all to see. He even daydreams of marrying Olivia and becoming a count. All the other characters dislike him, and it is easy to see why they do. Yet in recent times, actors, critics, and audiences have regarded Malvolio with more sympathy than Shakespeare may have intended. After all, he seems to be a man of honor and integrity, even if he is charmless. If he has no friends and inspires no affection, it is largely because he does his thankless duties so conscientiously. Fun-loving people are bound to find him disagreeable, especially a fun-loving character as irresponsible and parasitic as Sir Toby Belch.

Because the play involves the chaos that Twelfth Night festivities can produce, Malvolio must be punished for remaining so tightly bound to strict social mores. His social ambition, self-love, and desire to stick to protocol all doom him to his misfortune. However, Malvolio is a lonely figure, punished a little harshly for what are actually minor faults. Despite the necessity of his punishment, he becomes a pitiable character and even becomes noble in integrity. When Sir Toby confines him in the dark room, for example, Malvolio is sure enough to continue declaring his sanity, when everyone else states that he has gone mad.

Malvolio, alone, is punished for his love. Perhaps this is what makes him almost sympathetic to many audiences. Who of us, after all, could bear to have our daydreams revealed to the world as poor Malvolio's are?

At the end of the play, Malvolio is not even granted any apology for the scheme that has so humiliated him. He threatens revenge and stalks off the stage, leaving the only negative feeling in an otherwise happy ending.

Feste

Olivia's jester's very name (which is used only once in the entire play) suggests festivity, so it is no wonder that he and Malvolio are spiritual enemies. Feste, we learn, has returned to Olivia's household after a long and unexplained absence. Feste's humor is diverse: puns, playful insults, snatches of Latin, bogus quotations from fictitious ancient philosophers (whom he calls by such invented names as Quinapalus and Pigrogromitus), parodies, paradoxes, and other forms of whimsy. Many of his jokes seem deliberately obscure, and scholars have never agreed on what some of them mean (if indeed they mean anything). We must beware of assuming that Shakespeare's language was always easy for Elizabethan audiences to understand. It was not. At times, it must have been just as challenging for them as it is for us, and he meant it to be. The difficulty lies in the density, not just the period, of his language. Some of Shakespeare's finest and most admiring critics, such as Samuel Johnson, have complained that he is often needlessly obscure. (At times modern editors are unsure whether an obscure passage is what Shakespeare intended or is actually a misprint in the earliest edition!)

Feste quibbles constantly with the terms "fool," "folly," "wit," "wisdom," and "madness," noting that words may be abused to prove almost anything. He is not Olivia's fool, he insists, but her "corrupter of words." And he deplores the modern abuse of words: "To see this age! A sentence is but a cheveril [soft leather] glove to a good wit. How quickly the wrong side may be turned outward!" He laments that "words are grown so false, I am loath to prove reason with them."

In his own humorous way, Feste is a truth seeker. He faces himself without illusions. When Orsino asks him how he is doing, he gives the puzzling reply, "Truly, sir, the better for my foes, and the worse for my friends." Surely, Orsino says, you mean just the contrary: "the better for thy friends." No, says Feste; "they praise me and make an ass of me. Now my foes tell me plainly that I am an ass; so that by my foes, sir, I profit in the knowledge of myself, and by my friends I am abused [deceived]; . . . why then, the worse for my friends, and the better for my foes."

Sir Toby Belch

The name of Olivia's uncle seems to imply crudeness. He is a useless parasite—a glutton and drunkard—who lives shamelessly off others, including his niece and the dull-witted Sir Andrew.

The earthy Sir Toby is often likened to Sir John Falstaff (a character from Shakespeare's history plays), but the resemblance is largely on the surface. Falstaff is wittier and has a much deeper and warmer personality in contrast to Sir Toby, who is merely a clever and shallow cynic. Nobody would call Sir Toby, vivid and funny as he is, one of Shakespeare's greatest creations; he has none of that seemingly infinite inventiveness of such characters as Falstaff, Hamlet, Cleopatra, and even the diabolical Iago. We can hardly imagine him in another setting or another play. He is best known for a single memorable taunt at Malvolio: "Dost thou think, because thou art virtuous, there shall be no more cakes and ale?"

Sir Andrew Aguecheek

The well-to-do Sir Andrew, encouraged by Sir Toby, has come to woo Olivia, though he has no chance of winning her hand. He is stupid, as he himself is dimly aware: he observes, "Methinks sometimes I have no more wit than a Christian or an ordinary man has. But I am a great eater of beef, and I believe that does harm to my wit." He never suspects that Sir Toby is taking advantage of him for his money, and Sir Toby's jokes at his expense go right over his head.

Sir Andrew's vain desire for Olivia makes him one with two other failed suitors—Orsino and Malvolio—who also harbor dreams of possessing the rich countess until Sebastian suddenly appears and marries her. At the same time, Sebastian's valor in the duel scene exposes Sir Andrew's comical cowardice.

We may well wonder what sort of woman would want to marry Sir Andrew. Yet he does have a single good quality: his cheerful nature.

"O Time, Thou Must Untangle This"

Even Viola knows that the complexity of her situation is beyond her control. Only time, she says, will bring a resolution. Viola effectively captures the audience's experience with this admission. It takes time for each carefully wrought thread of the play to come together for the play's resolution.

Shakespeare's characters come to life, even on the page. Shakespeare masterfully creates a blend of complex characters and minor roles (like the sea captain and the musicians). The characters who populate Illyria make the kingdom feel real, too. One of Shakespeare's biggest strengths was creating inventive characters, though his labyrinthine plots receive more attention from critics.

Chapter Three

A Closer Look

S hakespeare wrote layered, intelligent plays. Even his slapstick comedies are of substance; all of Shakespeare's plays feature numerous literary devices and sophisticated plots. It is this sophistication that gives literary critics enough material for a lifetime of scholarship.

Twelfth Night is no exception. The twists and turns of the play's plot are underpinned by themes, symbols, and motifs that reinforce *Twelfth Night*'s message. Are people what they seem? How are men and women different? What makes someone fall in love? This chapter explores the elements of *Twelfth Night* that, together, create a resonant work of literature.

Themes

The Differences Between the Sexes

Twelfth Night's central character, Viola, the lovely girl disguised as a boy, combines both masculine and feminine virtues; so does her equally attractive twin brother, Sebastian. Shakespeare never suggests that the two sexes are interchangeable, however; he loves and delights in both as they are.

Anne Hathaway stars as Cesario/Viola in the 2014 *Twelfth Night* production performed at Central Park's Delacorte Theater in New York.

Important Literary Terms

IT'S IMPORTANT TO understand the terminology that scholars use when discussing plays, poems, and pieces of fiction. The following terms will help you to better understand not just *Twelfth Night* or Shakespeare's body of work but literature as a whole:

allegory A story in which characters and events stand for general moral truths. Shakespeare never uses this form simply, but his plays are full of allegorical elements.

alliteration Repetition of one or more initial sounds, especially consonants, as in the saying "through thick and thin," or in Julius Caesar's statement, "veni, vidi, vici."

allusion A reference, especially when the subject referred to is not actually named, but is unmistakably hinted at.

aside A short speech in which a character speaks to the audience, unheard by other characters on the stage.

comedy A story written to amuse, using devices such as witty dialogue (high comedy) or silly physical movement (low comedy). Most of Shakespeare's comedies were romantic comedies, incorporating lovers who endure separations, misunderstandings, and other obstacles but who are finally united in a happy resolution.

deus ex machina An unexpected, artificial resolution to a play's convoluted plot. Literally, "god out of a machine."

dialogue Speech that takes place among two or more characters.

diction Choice of words for tone. A speech's diction may be dignified (as when a king formally addresses his court), comic (as when the ignorant gravediggers debate whether Ophelia deserves a religious funeral), vulgar, romantic, or whatever the dramatic occasion requires. Shakespeare was a master of diction.

Elizabethan Having to do with the reign of Queen Elizabeth I, from 1558 until her death in 1603. This is considered the most famous period in the history of England, chiefly because of Shakespeare and other noted authors (among them Sir Philip Sidney, Edmund Spenser, and Christopher Marlowe). It was also an era of military glory, especially the defeat of the huge Spanish Armada in 1588.

hyperbole An excessively elaborate exaggeration used to create special emphasis or a comic effect, as in Montague's remark that his son Romeo's sighs are "adding to clouds more clouds" in Romeo and Juliet.

irony A discrepancy between what a character says and what he or she truly believes, what is expected to happen and what really happens, or between what a character says and what others understand.

metaphor A figure of speech in which one thing is identified with another, such as when Hamlet calls his father a "fair mountain." (See also simile.)

monologue A speech delivered by a single character.

motif A recurrent theme or image, such as disease in *Hamlet* or moonlight in *A Midsummer Night's Dream.*

oxymoron A phrase that combines two contradictory terms, as in the phrase "sounds of silence" or Hamlet's remark, "I must be cruel only to be kind."

personification Imparting personality to something impersonal ("the sky wept"); giving human qualities to an idea or an inanimate object, as in the saying "love is blind."

pun A playful treatment of words that sound alike, or are exactly the same, but have different meanings. In *Romeo and Juliet,* Mercutio says, after being fatally wounded, "Ask for me tomorrow and you shall find me a grave man." "Grave" could mean either a place of burial or serious.

simile A figure of speech in which one thing is compared to another, usually using the word like or as. (See also metaphor.)

soliloquy A speech delivered by a single character, addressed to the audience. The most famous are those of Hamlet, but Shakespeare uses this device frequently to tell us his characters' inner thoughts.

symbol A visible thing that stands for an invisible quality, as poison in Hamlet stands for evil and treachery.

syntax Sentence structure or grammar. Shakespeare displays amazing variety of syntax, from the sweet simplicity of his songs to the clotted fury of his great tragic heroes, who can be very difficult to understand at a first hearing. These effects are deliberate; if we are confused, it is because Shakespeare means to confuse us.

theme The abstract subject or message of a work of art, such as revenge in *Hamlet* or overweening ambition in *Macbeth.*

tone The style or approach of a work of art. The tone of *A Midsummer Night's Dream,* set by the lovers, Bottom's crew, and the fairies, is light and sweet. The tone of *Macbeth,* set by the witches, is dark and sinister.

tragedy A story that traces a character's fall from power, sanity, or privilege. Shakespeare's well-known tragedies include *Hamlet, Macbeth,* and *Othello.*

tragicomedy A story that combines elements of both tragedy and comedy, moving a heavy plot through twists and turns to a happy ending.

verisimilitude Having the appearance of being real or true.

understatement A statement expressing less than intended, often with an ironic or comic intention; the opposite of hyperbole.

What is most surprising to modern scholars is how little Shakespeare relies on gender stereotypes, particularly for the character of Viola. Viola is not only capable because she is disguised as a man but, rather, she is an intelligent woman who can outwit most of the men in the play (and can do so while dressed in masculine clothing). Maria, too, is a witty and sly woman who hatches a devious plot against Malvolio. While romantic love underpins the entire plot, Shakespeare seems to be suggesting that balance between lovers and friends is more important than anything else.

Instead of stereotypical differences between men and women, the play is much more concerned with wit and wisdom, on the one hand, and folly and madness on the other. It insists that fools and wise men (or women) are not always easy to tell apart.

The Elusiveness of Truth

Viola is basically honest. She adopts a disguise only to protect herself in a strange country, not to take advantage of others. She tells the truth as much as possible, often indirectly, as when she tells Orsino of her fictitious sister who "never told her love," in effect describing her own secret love for Orsino. Feste the jester tells the truth indirectly too, in jokes, riddles, and parodies of scholarship, as when he playfully quotes an "old hermit of Prague, that never saw pen and ink, [who] very wittily said to a niece of King Gorboduc, 'That that is, is.'" The impish Feste does this sort of thing constantly. As the discerning Viola says of him, "This fellow is wise enough to play the fool."

Disguises and Ruses

The play is full of deceits, disguises, and playful conspiracies. Viola deceives nearly everyone with her

Cesario disguise. Maria, Sir Toby, and Fabian fool Malvolio with a forged letter; later, Feste joins the fun by impersonating a priest. Sir Toby tricks Sir Andrew out of his money and then lures him into a duel with Cesario.

Antonio, a sea captain, mistakenly thinks Cesario/Viola is his friend Sebastian, whom he has befriended at great risk to himself and appears to have betrayed him. All these blunders are eventually resolved in concord, without tragedy.

Viola's identical twin brother, Sebastian, is mistaken for her; the results include a violent duel and a happy marriage to Olivia, who is enamored of Cesario, the boy she believes Viola to be. Duke (or is he a count?) Orsino, meanwhile, upon learning that Cesario is actually a girl, falls in love with her and weds her.

Of course, these playful ruses and topsy-turvy roles are all a part of the Twelfth Night festivities. At the end of the play, order is restored to the chaos allowed during Twelfth Night. But these role reversals are not all for nothing. They teach the characters about themselves, which allows the characters their happy endings. (The only character who refuses to have any fun, or adopt any ruse knowingly, Malvolio, has the most unhappy ending.)

Motifs

Word Play

Several of the characters of *Twelfth Night* love word play. They cite Latin phrases, supposed ancient authors, and other fragments of humorous "learning." Sir Toby and Feste specialize in such word games, which are funny because they are usually so inappropriate to the occasion of their use; Feste—the self-styled "corrupter of words"—

laments the abuse of language but then deliberately abuses it himself, just for fun. Malvolio disapproves of Feste's whimsical humor and, as we should expect, belittles and insults it. Sir Toby would enliven any celebration; but Malvolio, it seems safe to say, would be the death of the party.

Madness

Madness, or possible madness, also permeates the play. While no character is truly mad, madness is either feigned or suspected. Olivia believes Malvolio to be mad, when he is really just acting out the directions offered in the forged letter. Malvolio's confusion when he is locked in the room following his strange behavior leads him to believe everyone else is mad but him. At the end of the play, when Antonio mistakes Viola for Sebastian, Viola and the other characters believe him to be mad, too. The prevalence of madness throughout the play shows the fine line between madness and sanity during periods of chaos. As with gender difference, Shakespeare hints that the distinction between madness and sanity might not be as cut-and-dried as it seems.

Symbols

As it so often does, water stands for disparate and even conflicting things: it can be both a nourisher and a destroyer of life. The sea produces the shipwreck that nearly drowns both Viola and Sebastian, casting both of them up on the coast of Illyria; yet Orsino, in the play's first speech, likens the sea to the spirit of love.

Darkness is also an important symbol in the play. The lack of light in Malvolio's prison is a symbol for the

Mark Rylance, as Olivia, and Stephen Fry, as Malvolio, in the Apollo Theater in London, England

darkness of his understanding. He cannot understand why the other characters are behaving as if he were mad, just as the other characters cannot understand Malvolio's strange change in behavior (except for those, of course, who came up with the ruse in the first place). Malvolio even states, "I say this house is as dark as ignorance, though ignorance were as dark as hell."

Language

In this, one of Shakespeare's most charming works, his mastery of the English language is more casual than usual, with little of the spectacular eloquence of the great tragedies, but an easygoing assurance that makes the dialogue memorable. Even the names of the characters are suggestive: Malvolio is apt for a villain (though not everyone agrees that he is a villain), and Feste hints at festivity. Sir Toby Belch is suitably crude, as his name implies; he is hardly a refined or chivalrous specimen of knighthood. Viola is a delicate, flowerlike beauty—one of Shakespeare's most beloved heroines.

Consider a few of the play's most famous lines: Orsino's "If music be the food of love, play on," which opens the play; Sir Toby's "Dost thou think, because thou art virtuous, there shall be no more cakes and ale?"; Sir Andrew's sublime line "I am a great eater of beef, and I believe that does harm to my wit"; Olivia's "Why, this is very midsummer madness"; the forged letter's "Some are born great, some achieve greatness, and some have greatness thrust upon them"; and many more. These are all common lines, still in use today, none of them relying on the Bard's awesome vocabulary for their effect. Shakespeare's simple good humor suffices. And all this does not even include the wondrous little songs, those plain and immortally haunting love ditties, written in monosyllables, which no other genius could have conceived.

Interpreting the Play

Most scholars believe that *Twelfth Night* was written within a couple of years of *Julius Caesar*. If so, this fact illustrates the incredible range and versatility of Shakespeare's imagination, for it would be hard to name two plays so different as the romantic comedy set in the fantasy land of Illyria and the solemn historical tragedy of ancient Rome.

If the tragic plot seems driven by powerful, flawed characters, the plot of comedy seems determined by gentler forces: divine providence, supernatural intervention (think of Oberon, Titania, and Puck), magic or miracles (as in *The Tempest*), good luck, mere accident, or happy coincidence.

This 1900 illustration by Otto Printz shows Olivia and Viola in Olivia's garden.

Excavating the Curtain Theatre

THE GLOBE WASN'T Shakespeare's only theater. The Curtain Theatre was the second playhouse opened in greater London, inaugurated in 1577. In 1597, before the Globe Theatre was built, it became the top venue for Shakespeare's acting troupe, called the Lord Chamberlain's Men. There, some of Shakespeare's most famous plays, such as *Romeo and Juliet* and *Henry V,* were first staged. In fact, in the prologue to *Henry V*, the Curtain itself is referred to and is described as "the wooden O." (Many theaters at the time, including the Globe Theatre, were circular in shape.) The theater was only used by Shakespeare's troupe for two years. In 1599, the Lord Chamberlain's Men moved to the Globe Theatre. But plays were continually performed at the Curtain, at least until 1624 when the theater appeared to close down—for what reason, scholars are still unsure.

In 2012, archeologists discovered the original spot of the Curtain and began excavations there. What they found surprised many Shakespearean experts. In 2016, they announced that—contrary to popular belief—the theater was not circular as had previously been believed. The Curtain was a rectangular playhouse that was built to house about one thousand people. What about the reference to the "wooden O"? Scholars now surmise that the prologue was added after its initial production at the Curtain.

Archaeologists dig at the site of the Curtain Theatre in 2016.

Excavations will continue at the Curtain for the foreseeable future. Archeologists have preserved the theater's foundations for public view and are conducting tours for the four-hundredth anniversary of Shakespeare's death. Other discoveries have been unearthed at the Curtain, too, including a sixteenth-century bird whistle that may have been used in the famous scene in *Romeo and Juliet* where Juliet convinces her lover that the sound they just heard was not a lark, but a nightingale.

The tragic hero typically brings his fate on himself. Even if he does not exactly deserve the disaster he helps to provoke, it has a certain fitness to his character, whether he is an evildoer like Macbeth or an essentially noble soul like Othello. In *Twelfth Night*, Viola is both a virtuous character and a very lucky one: she and her twin brother, Sebastian, both survive a shipwreck, and everything turns out happily for her. Even Sebastian's abrupt and unforeseeable marriage to Olivia is part of Viola's good fortune. In real life we would feel that such a marriage was rash and unwise, but in comedy we can be confident that everything will turn out all right. Comedy naturally moves toward marriage, joy, and festivity ... "And they lived happily ever after."

In its early scenes, *Twelfth Night* touches briefly on the subject of death, but none of the characters we see are ever in real danger of dying. Illyria is a Never-Never Land where fate is a kindly force and serious evil can hardly exist. We feel that tragedy is impossible there. If Malvolio can be called the play's villain, he is quite a harmless villain, and despite his name (which means "ill will"), he is not even malicious. In fact, he is the dupe and victim of the other characters, who make him their sport almost from the beginning. If his chief fault is, as Olivia says, "self-love," then his punishment is no worse than frustration and humiliation.

Far from illuminating readers, much of the modern criticism of *Twelfth Night* has been harder to understand than the play itself. In 1818, the great William Hazlitt offered the surprising opinion that the play is "perhaps too good-natured for comedy." A few years later, another famous commentator, Charles Lamb, wrote a noted

Actors from the Lions Part group perform during a Twelfth Night celebration in London, mixing ancient and modern customs.

defense of the character of Malvolio, denying that the Bard meant him to be a mere comic butt, but on the contrary gave him real dignity.

The play's title refers to the final night of the traditional Christmas season, the Feast of the Epiphany, and it is clear that the play's setting is Christian (even though some of the characters appeal to such pagan gods as Jove and Mercury): we hear of churches, a chantry, heaven and hell, fiends, and devils, and the characters include both a real and a fake priest.

And yet even this sweet and charming play has undertones of sadness and grief. Its first scene tells us of mourning, it has many references (both literal and figurative) to drowning, and its final lines remind us that "the rain it raineth every day."

Shakespeare and Our World

Though it was written sometime between 1600 and 1602, in many ways *Twelfth Night* feels modern. The issues Shakespeare tackles—especially the roles of the sexes—continue to affect contemporary experience. Viola leads readers to question stereotypes about women. Malvolio inspires debate about ambition and social status. Feste makes us question whether a "fool" can be wise. The pranks of Maria, Sir Toby, Sir Andrew, and Fabian raise ethical questions: How far is too far? Does Malvolio deserve his comeuppance?

These are the questions that audiences have weighed for the last four centuries. Their answers are hotly debated, and it's often impossible to reach a consensus among people. In this way, Shakespeare's play serves as a litmus test for an individual's deep-seated values. There are no correct answers; Shakespeare's plays operate in the gray area between wrong and right. Uncertainty, confusion, and evolving values characterize *Twelfth Night*. Thus, the play is like life itself. And this is the secret to Shakespeare's enduring success: he holds a mirror to our lives and lets us work out the complicated reflection for ourselves.

Of course, *Twelfth Night*'s staying power is also related to the fact that it's wickedly funny. The comic circumstances penned by Shakespeare are just as funny today as they were when the play was first performed in 1602. It's nearly impossible not to laugh as Malvolio enters dressed in a ridiculous outfit or when Sir Toby orchestrates a comical duel between Cesario and Sir Andrew.

Twelfth Night's motifs, themes, and symbols both provide depth and further the plot. Think of how Viola bends the truth without really lying. Her wordplay is the foundation of her successful ruse. Her wit is the reason for her happy ending—and her twin brother's, as well.

Like the Twelfth Night festivities themselves, the play is worth celebrating.

CHRONOLOGY

1564 William Shakespeare is born on April 23 in Stratford-upon-Avon, England.

1578–1582 Span of Shakespeare's "Lost Years," covering the time between leaving school and marrying Anne Hathaway of Stratford.

1582 At age eighteen Shakespeare marries Anne Hathaway, age twenty-six, on November 28.

1583 Susanna Shakespeare, William and Anne's first child, is born in May, six months after the wedding.

1584 Birth of twins Hamnet and Judith Shakespeare.

1585–1592 Shakespeare leaves his family in Stratford to become an actor and playwright in a London theater company.

1587 Public beheading of Mary, Queen of Scots.

1593–1594 The Bubonic (Black) Plague closes theaters in London.

1594–1596 As a leading playwright, Shakespeare creates some of his most popular work, including *A Midsummer Night's Dream* and *Romeo and Juliet*.

1596 Hamnet Shakespeare dies in August at age eleven, possibly of plague.

1596–1597 *The Merchant of Venice* and *Henry IV, Part One* most likely are written.

1599 The Globe Theatre opens.

1600 *Julius Caesar* is first performed at the Globe.

1600–1601 *Hamlet* is believed to have been written.

1600–1602 *Twelfth Night* is probably composed.

1603 Queen Elizabeth dies; Scottish king James VI succeeds her and becomes England's James I.

1604 Shakespeare pens *Othello*.

1605 *Macbeth* is composed.

1608–1610 London's theaters are forced to close when the plague returns and kills an estimated thirty-three thousand people.

1611 *The Tempest* is written.

1613 The Globe Theatre is destroyed by fire.

1614 Reopening of the Globe.

1616 Shakespeare dies on April 23.

1623 Anne Hathaway, Shakespeare's widow, dies; a collection of Shakespeare's plays, known as the First Folio, is published.

A SHAKESPEARE GLOSSARY

addition A name or title, such as knight, duke, duchess, king, etc.

affect To like or love; to be attracted to.

approve To prove or confirm.

attend To pay attention.

belike Probably.

beseech To beg or request.

bondman A slave.

bootless Futile; useless; in vain.

broil A battle.

charge Expense, responsibility; to command or accuse.

common A term describing the common people, below nobility.

condition Social rank; quality.

countenance Face; appearance; favor.

cousin A relative.

curious Careful; attentive to detail.

discourse To converse; conversation.

discover To reveal or uncover.

dispatch To speed or hurry; to send; to kill.

doubt To suspect.

entreat To beg or appeal.

envy To hate or resent; hatred; resentment.

ere Before.

eyne Eyes.

fain Gladly.

fare To eat; to prosper.

favor Face, privilege.

fellow A peer or equal.

filial Of a child toward its parent.

fine An end; "in fine" means in sum.

folio A book made up of individually printed sheets, each folded in half to make four pages; Shakespeare's folios contain all of his known plays in addition to other works.

fond Foolish.

fool A darling.

genius A good or evil spirit.

gentle Well-bred; not common.

gentleman One whose labor was done by servants. (Note: to call someone a gentleman was not a mere compliment on his manners; it meant that he was above the common people.)

gentles People of quality.

get To beget (a child).

go to "Go on"; "come off it."

go we Let us go.

haply Perhaps.

happily By chance; fortunately.

hard by Nearby.

heavy Sad or serious.

husbandry Thrift; economy.

instant Immediate.

kind One's nature; species.

knave A villain; a poor man.

lady A woman of high social rank. (Note: lady was not a synonym for woman or polite woman; it was not a compliment but simply a word referring to one's actual legal status in society, like gentleman.)

leave Permission; "take my leave" means depart (with permission).

lief, lieve "I had as lief " means I would just as soon; I would rather.

like To please; "it likes me not" means it is disagreeable to me.

livery The uniform of a nobleman's servants; emblem.

Lord Chamberlain's Men The company of players Shakespeare joined in London; under James I they became the King's Men.

mark Notice; pay attention.

morrow Morning.

needs Necessarily.

nice Too fussy or fastidious.

owe To own.

passing Very.

peculiar Individual; exclusive.

privy Private; secret.

proper Handsome; one's very own ("his proper son").

protest To insist or declare.

quite Completely.

require Request.

several Different, various.

severally Separately.

sirrah A term used to address social inferiors.

sooth Truth.

state Condition; social rank.

still Always; persistently.

success Result(s).

surfeit Fullness.

touching Concerning; about; as for.

translate To transform.

unfold To disclose.

verse Writing that uses a regular metrical rhythm and is divided from other lines by a space.

villain A low or evil person; originally, a peasant.

voice A vote; consent; approval.

vouchsafe To confide or grant.

vulgar Common.

want To lack.

SUGGESTED ESSAY TOPICS

1. Discuss the elements of sadness and melancholy in *Twelfth Night*.

2. Is Malvolio the villain of *Twelfth Night*? Why or why not?

3. Compare and contrast Sir Toby Belch and Sir John Falstaff.

4. How does Feste view the other characters of *Twelfth Night*?

5. *Twelfth Night* ends with Orsino hoping to mollify Malvolio. Is this likely to happen? Why or why not?

TEST YOUR MEMORY

1. How long does Olivia intend to mourn her dead brother? a) a year; b) a month; c) forever; d) seven years.

2. Viola's original plan is to disguise herself as a) a boy; b) a knight; c) a sailor; d) a eunuch.

3. Sir Toby is Olivia's a) steward; b) wooer; c) uncle; d) jester.

4. Sir Andrew has come to Olivia's household in the hope of a) getting rich; b) marrying her; c) reveling; d) dancing.

5. Sir Andrew is supposedly skilled in a) speaking foreign languages; b) fencing; c) charming the opposite sex; d) playing chess.

6. To what does Sir Andrew attribute his own weak wit? a) beef; b) drinking; c) idleness; d) bad company.

7. How long does it take Viola to win Orsino's full confidence? a) an hour; b) a week; c) three days; d) three months.

8. Feste has just returned from a) a journey to Italy; b) an unexplained absence; c) exile; d) England.

9. Quinapalus is a) a kinsman of Orsino;
b) a sea captain; c) an ancient Roman warrior;
d) an imaginary philosopher.

10. What is Malvolio's attitude toward Feste? a) affection;
b) resentment; c) contempt; d) jealousy.

11. Sebastian and Viola are a) lovers; b) enemies;
c) twins; d) old friends.

12. When we first meet Sebastian, his chief interest is a)
Viola's fate; b) Olivia's dowry; c) Sir Andrew's wealth;
d) Orsino's dukedom.

13. Maria scornfully likens Malvolio to a) a pickpocket;
b) a puritan; c) a police agent; d) a politician.

14. Malvolio is deceived by a) a lie; b) the twins;
c) a messenger from Orsino; d) a forged letter.

15. Who does Malvolio think wrote the letter to him?
a) Maria; b) Viola; c) Rosalind; d) Olivia.

16. Name the source of these famous words: "Some are
born great, some achieve greatness, and some have
greatness thrust upon 'em." a) Viola; b) Sir Toby;
c) Malvolio; d) Maria.

17. Who risks his life to help Sebastian?
a) Antonio; b) Feste; c) Orsino; d) Cesario.

18. Sir Topas is a) a drinking companion of Sir Toby
and Sir Andrew; b) Feste in the disguise of a priest; c)
Orsino's bodyguard; d) a steward.

19. Who finally marries Olivia? a) Sebastian; b) Cesario;
c) Orsino; d) Sir Andrew.

20. Whom does Maria finally marry? a) Malvolio;
b) Sir Toby; c) Feste; d) Fabian.

Answer Key

1.) d; 2.) d; 3.) c; 4.) b; 5.) a; 6.) a; 7.) c; 8.) b; 9.) d; 10.) c;
11.) c; 12.) a; 13.) b; 14.) d; 15.) d; 16.) d; 17.) a; 18.) b; 19.) a; 20.) b

FURTHER INFORMATION

Books

Johnson, Boris. *Shakespeare: The Riddle of Genius.* New York: Riverhead Books, 2016.

Mulherin, Jennifer. *Shakespeare for Everyone: Twelfth Night.* Weybridge, Vermont: Cherry Tree Books, 2016.

Shakespeare, William. *Twelfth Night.* New York: Macmillan Collector's Library, 2016.

Van Es, Bart. *Shakespeare's Comedies: A Very Short Introduction.* Oxford, England: Oxford University Press, 2016.

Websites

Absolute Shakespeare

http://www.absoluteshakespeare.com

Absolute Shakespeare is a resource for the Bard's plays, sonnets, and poems and includes summaries, quotes, films, trivia, and more.

Play Shakespeare: The Ultimate
Free Shakespeare Resource
http://www.playshakespeare.com

This website features full-text versions of Shakespeare's plays along with an online glossary, reviews, a discussion forum, and links to festivals worldwide.

The Shakespeare Resource Center
http://www.bardweb.net

The Shakespeare Resource Center provides a vast collection of links to assist in online research; click on Ask the Bard for "burning questions."

Shakespeare's Globe: Globe Player
http://www.globeplayer.tv

In 2015, Shakespeare's Globe released the Globe Player, the first on-demand website for Globe productions, in order to make Shakespeare's work more accessible to people around the world.

DVD

Twelfth Night–Shakespeare's Globe Theatre on Screen, directed by Tim Carroll; with Stephen Fry, Mark Rylance, et al., 2015.

CD

Shakespeare in Music and Words, Paul Hardwick, Derek Godfrey, Dorothy Tutin, et al., Decca, 2016.

BIBLIOGRAPHY

Bate, Jonathan, and Eric Rasmussen, eds. *William Shakespeare Complete Works (Modern Library)*. New York: Random House, 2007.

Bloom, Harold. *Shakespeare: The Invention of the Human*. New York: Riverhead Books, 1998.

Burgess, Anthony. *Shakespeare*. New York: Alfred A. Knopf, 1970.

Chute, Marchette. *Shakespeare of London*. New York: Dutton, 1949.

Garber, Marjorie. *Shakespeare After All*. New York: Pantheon, 2004.

Goddard, Harold C. *The Meaning of Shakespeare*. Chicago: University of Chicago Press, 1951.

Greenblatt, Stephen. *Will in the World: How Shakespeare Became Shakespeare*. New York: W. W. Norton & Company, 2004.

Honan, Park. *Shakespeare: A Life*. New York: Clarendon Press, 1998.

Schoenbaum, Samuel. *William Shakespeare: A Documentary Life*. New York: Oxford University Press, 1975.

———. *William Shakespeare: Records and Images*. New York: Oxford University Press, 1981.

Traversi, D. A. *An Approach to Shakespeare.* Palo Alto, CA: Stanford University Press, 1957.

Van Doren, Mark. *Shakespeare.* Garden City, NY: Doubleday, 1939.

INDEX

ABOUT THE AUTHORS

Elizabeth Schmermund is a writer, scholar, and editor. Her favorite of Shakespeare's plays is *A Midsummer Night's Dream*, although she also loves *Twelfth Night*. Schmermund lives with her husband and young son in New York.

Dale Robeson has worked as a journalist, a technical writer, and most recently, as a librarian at a high school. Robeson travels widely and visiting Stratford-upon-Avon was a trip to remember.